Welcome to the
dixiechicks
Photo Biography

dixiechicks

The publication of *The Dixie Chicks*
has been generously supported by
the Government of Canada through the
Book Publishing Industry Development Program.

CANADIAN CATALOGUING IN PUBLICATION DATA

ISBN 1-55022-418-2
1. Dixie Chicks. 2. Country musicians — United States — Biography. I. Title.
ML421.D619T76 2000   782.421642'092'2   C00-931706-6

Cover and interior design by Guylaine Régimbald.
This book is set in CgEuropa and Sari.

Printed by Printcrafters Inc., Winnipeg, Canada.

Distributed in Canada by General Distribution Services,
325 Humber College Blvd., Etobicoke, Ontario M9W 7C3.

Distributed in the United States by LPC Group,
1436 West Randolph Street, Chicago, Illinois, 60607. U.S.A.

Distributed in Europe by Turnaround Publisher Services, Unit 3,
Olympia Trading Estate, Coburg Road, Wood Green, London N2Z 6T2

Distributed in Australia and New Zealand by Wakefield Press
17 Rundle Street (Box 2266), Kent Town, South Australia 5071

Published by ECW PRESS,
2120 Queen Street East, Suite 200,
Toronto, Ontario M4E 1E2.

ecwpress.com

PRINTED AND BOUND IN CANADA

ECW *Press*

These days "grrrl power" comes with a country twang and is accompanied by a bluegrass melody. While the Spice Girls may have made the music world safe for girl groups again, it's the Dixie Chicks who are almost single-handedly reinventing a classic country sound—and, in the process, emerging as some of Nashville's brightest stars of the future. Not only do country purists enjoy their traditional roots, but their modern take on the music is also drawing in new fans—people who had previously considered country the domain of women with big hair and men in shiny suits. Ironically, the trio who are now making country safe for Top 40 radio began their careers with a look more reminiscent of Tammy Wynette than Shania Twain; and the story of how the Dixie Chicks evolved from a local band into one of the music industry's most unique acts is a tale straight out of an old-time country song.

Although Martie and Em might seem as down home as grits, they were actually born in Pittsfield, Massachusetts. They are the second and third daughters, respectively, of schoolteachers Paul and Barbara Erwin. Martha was born on October 12, 1969, followed by Emily, three years later, on August 16, 1972. Shortly after Em's birth, the Erwins packed up Martie, Em, and their older sister, Julie, and moved to Dallas, Texas. Despite their new, southern surroundings, country music wasn't an Erwin family staple. Instead, Paul and Barbara introduced their children to the music of the local symphony. "We took them to the symphony and bribed them to

The story begins with the Erwin sisters

sit still by promising we would take them out to breakfast," Barbara would later say. The Erwins believed that exposure to classical music was an important part of a child's education. So was learning to play an instrument: when they were still young children, Martie and Em both took violin lessons. But, while their parents may have had visions of them playing the great symphony halls, their musical leanings were earthier. Although the girls enjoyed classical music, what really struck a chord with them was what they heard when their dad took them to see country-music performances. Fortunately, Paul and Barbara were not musical snobs, and they encouraged their daughters' passion.

Although Martie was an accomplished musician by any standard, Emily was becoming a one-woman band. In addition to playing the violin, she also learned to play a variety of other instruments, including bass, rhythm guitar, banjo, and dobro. By the time Martie began attending Greenhill High School, where Barbara was an English teacher, she and Em were spending most weekends competing in fiddle contests all over the state of Texas.

Sometimes they even played hooky. As teenagers, the girls would skip school every year to attend the Walnut Valley Festival in Winfield, Kansas, along with some friends, a brother and sister named Sharon and Troy Gilcrist, who also loved bluegrass. According to an acquaintance, "Troy learned to flat-pick the guitar before he was really big enough to reach all the way around the monstrous instrument and Sharon knew as many mandolin chops as just about anyone attending the festival." Together the four would listen to music and daydream about becoming professional musicians. The teens were occasionally invited to play with some of the festival performers, such as Mark O'Connor.

Intent on taking advantage of the opportunity, Martie, Em, Sharon, and Troy would borrow some of the melodies they were hearing and rearrange them to fit their own style and sound. Eventually, in 1984, the foursome started a band called Blue Night Express, and with that, the Erwin sisters' professional careers were launched. Blue Night Express became a popular local band in Dallas. Martie and Em provided lead vocals in addition to playing their instruments. When they weren't performing Martie, Em, Sharon, and Troy continued to take lessons, and they rehearsed religiously, always looking for new ways to enrich their music. In 1987, Martie placed second at the Walnut Valley Fiddle Championships, a contest that attracted some of the brightest young musicians around—such as Alison Krauss, who won the competition in 1984.

By the time Martie had graduated from high school and Emily was fifteen, Blue Night Express was performing at festivals and entering contests not only in Texas but also throughout the Midwest. What was particularly unique about the group was the youth of its members —at that time, bluegrass was considered by many to be a sound fancied by older genera-tions. The fact that this group of trained teenaged musicians embraced the bluegrass tradition set them apart from their contemporaries and breathed life into the genre.

But, regardless of their shared passion for bluegrass, Martie and Emily were not content to limit their musical horizons. Although they loved the sound and would continue

to incorporate it into their music, they did not want to be labeled as bluegrass performers. They also knew that if they really wanted to make a career of music they had to expand their repertoire; although the genre is a popular one on the festival circuit, only an extremely small percentage of bluegrass performers can make a living at it. So, while they continued to perform with Blue Night Express, both girls knew they would soon be obliged to move on.

In some ways it was inevitable that the group would disband and its members would follow separate paths—if for no other reason than the four were growing up. By 1989, Troy and Sharon had graduated from college; Martie was attending Southern Methodist University, where she was studying musical theory; and Em was juggling her high-school studies,

weekend performances, and weekday lessons and practices. In the most amicable way, Blue Night Express disbanded, and the Erwin sisters arrived at what would prove to be the turning point in their lives. Still, for awhile Em actually believed her days as a performer were over. "I never expected to get back into a band," she admits, "because I wanted to study hard and get into the Air Force Academy and become a pilot." Emily went so far as to fill out applications for the academy—then she realized that her math and science grades weren't good enough. So music won by default.

Thanks to Blue Night Express, Martie and Em had become well-known and well-respected bluegrass-circuit performers. Their harmonies and musicianship earned them the admiration of their peers, including a performer named Robin Lynn Macy. Robin had dabbled in music as a teenager in Missouri but then went off to college with the idea of becoming a lawyer. Once there, however, she switched to math. Shortly after graduating Robin moved to Dallas with hopes of rekindling her musical career. She drifted into doing some stage work, but all the while she longed to be performing musically.

Eventually she fell in with a group of local musicians and began attending jam sessions. This led to an invitation to join a band called Danger in the Air, a regular on the bluegrass festival circuit. But Robin was still earning very little money. So, in order to support herself, she worked as a sixth-grade math teacher at St. Mark's School for a couple of years. One of her former students recalls that she would sometimes play bluegrass for the kids in her class. She also continued to jam with other musicians, and one day she found herself playing with Emily and Martie Erwin. Despite the age difference—Robin was more than ten years older than Em and Martie—the three hit it off personally as well as

musically. Robin thought enough of the girls to ask them to jam with Danger in the Air. One night they all did a session at Uncle Calvin's Coffeehouse inside North Park Presbyterian Church.

Robin Lynn Macy and the Erwin sisters' relationship was deepening at a time when all three were facing career changes. As Blue Night Express was winding down, the high hopes that Robin had held for Danger in the Air were slowly ebbing away. The group had cut two self-produced albums—*Danger in the Air* and *Airtight*—neither of which generated enough enthusiasm among music-industry power brokers to propel the group to the next

level. When it became clear that none of the major labels was interested, Robin's tenure with Danger in the Air was essentially over. But she already had another idea for a band, and she approached Martie and Em about joining musical forces.

Erwin family friend Jane Frost says, "I'll never forget the night I was privy to the brand-new Chicks and their attitudes on what might or might not happen with the group. 'We think it might do well,' Martha pointed out." Frost also remembers Robin saying, boldly, "I can tell you one thing, it's going to be a *hot* band." Although she was the youngest Emily seemed the most pragmatic: "I give it six months and if we aren't making money by then, I'm out of here."

Robin had another card to play to help ensure their financial prospects, and her name was Laura Lynch. Having grown up on a West Texas cattle ranch, Laura attended the University of Texas and spent some time working in El Paso doing TV news. She divorced her husband shortly after the birth of their daughter and moved to Houston, where she worked as a stockbroker and was employed by a real-estate developer. But her career aspirations were decidedly not white collar. In her spare time Laura took guitar lessons and attended bluegrass festivals. It was at a festival in Nacogdoches in the late 1980s that she met Robin Lynn Macy.

By then Laura was living in Dallas and had already made a name for herself on the bluegrass circuit, playing with the Texas Rangers, a band that toured extensively both nationally and overseas. In addition to Laura, the group included Dave Peters and Marvin Gruenbaum. Although Laura was earning enough money playing with the Texas Rangers to support herself, life on the road was both physically grueling and emotionally taxing; it was particularly hard being away from her daughter. So when Robin approached her about starting up an all-girl band, Laura agreed to check it out.

At the time, all-girl bands were more of a pop thing than a country tradition, so Robin and the others suspected that more conservative country fans would be put off by their project. But the bigger question on the minds of Martie and Em was whether or not their styles would mesh harmoniously

with those of Laura and Robin. So, in order to find the answers to both questions, the foursome decided to set up on a street corner in Dallas's West End and see what kind of response they got. Not only were the cash donations surprisingly good, but also a barbecue place down the street offered the girls free eats if they would play three one-hour sets a night. With each impromptu performance, Martie and Em became convinced that they had found something special. Robin dubbed it "group female harmony." It was time for the group to come up with a name.

"When we made up the name, we were playing on the street corner for maybe fifty bucks at a time," Martie recalls. "People were saying, 'What's your name?'" The answer occurred to them when the Little Feat song "Dixie Chickens" came on the radio. Like a sign from the musical gods, the name seemed to capture their essence—almost. Upon reflection, the girls decided to shorten it to the less poultry-esque "Dixie Chicks." Although the name was definitely chosen with tongue-in-cheek whimsy, Martie adds, "once we did get legitimate gigs we couldn't think of a better name."

However, as it happened, "Dixie Chicks" seemed a particularly apt name because it reflected their early sound, which Martie describes as "an acoustic, nostalgic Western cowgirl sound." Martie (then still a redhead) and Emily played backup for lead singers Laura and Robin. In keeping with Robin's vision for the group the women also wore kitschy, bead-laden, fringed cowgirl costumes and reveled in big hair—an homage to a bygone musical era.

Still, as the group became better known, their name did present a problem. "I worry about our image for new people," admitted Martie. She was concerned that people wouldn't "get" the name "like our other fans got it. It's not supposed to be taken seriously."

Many on the bluegrass circuit who knew the four musicians as individuals were surprised to learn that they had joined creative forces. Music promoter Leo Eilits of Sante Fe Trails Productions remembers being at the 1989 Walnut Valley Festival when "these four gorgeous women, who I knew separately, showed up together at our campsite, Stage Six,

and announced that they had formed a band. They had about six songs worked up, and they played them for us under the big tent that serves as the common area of our campground. Laura played my bass, which was too tall for her, and we have a picture of her standing on an egg crate while they performed for us that afternoon."

       Eilits continues, "When Bob Redford, the festival promoter, came by the next afternoon and mentioned that he had an open stage slot if we had someone we wanted to put on, I suggested the Dixie Chicks. When I told the girls that I had scheduled them on a stage, Laura promptly threw up. When it finally came time to play, she was so nervous that my brother and I agreed to go on with them and play guitar and bass so that they

could concentrate on their singing. To my knowledge, that was their first appearance as a band in a festival setting."

The group's street-corner days didn't last long. They rapidly developed a fervent local following. Even so, it would be a couple more years before Robin felt confident enough that the Dixie Chicks would make it to quit her teaching job and devote herself completely to her music. Although the Chicks were steadily gaining fan support, it took awhile for them to command an actual salary instead of just playing for the cover charge. By the early 1990s, however, the Dixie Chicks were earning $2,500 or more per show. Their unique style coupled with their unbridled enthusiasm for the music prompted one club owner—

David Card, who ran Poor David's Pub—to comment, "They have a good chance if they're properly managed and make the right choices along the way in terms of music, booking, and people. I don't know what those choices are, but the road to musical success is littered with people who made the wrong choices."

Yet it seemed at that point like the Dixie Chicks could do no wrong—at least as far as their audience was concerned. Their unique arrangements of old standards such as "I Want to Be a Cowboy's Sweetheart"—complete with yodeling—captured the imagination of the audience and gave the material a fresh new dimension. They also performed original compositions, the most popular of which was a ditty called "Thank Heavens for Dale Evans," written by Martie, Robin, and a third collaborator named Lisa Brandenburg. The tribute was appropriate: the Dixie Chicks' look was reminiscent of Dale Evans in her cowgirl prime.

With their status as a hometown favorite established, the time was ripe for the Chicks to cut their first album. But they suddenly found themselves in a bit of a Nashville catch-22. Their local popularity was built on their retro look and their choice of material, yet those things were precisely what caused the eyes of record-label executives to glaze over. By the early 1990s country music was going through an evolution. The genre split into factions: young country performers, who were attracting a large crossover pop audience; and the traditionalists, who felt that the music of the younger performers wasn't pure country. But the sales figures that these young acts—such as Garth Brooks—were ringing up were music to label executives' ears. They were anxious to sign artists who could bring in new fans. As a result, fewer and fewer country-music stations were playing a cross-section of country genres, concentrating instead on the younger, pop-influenced, top-selling acts. Country radio began to sound like Top 40 with a twang.

It was in this atmosphere that the Dixie Chicks made their first album. The project had a different significance for Laura and Robin than it did for the Erwin sisters. For Laura and Robin the album was an almost purely artistic endeavor; their aim was to promote bluegrass, and they had no intention of compromising the material to boost its commercial appeal. Martie and Emily considered making the album as much a learning experience as an artistic endeavor.

It's ironic that the Dixie Chicks' image at this time belied the musicianship of the group's individual members, particularly Martie and Emily. While outsiders may have begun to see the group as a novelty act, along the lines of Weird Al Yankovich, they remained united by the seriousness with which they regarded their music, even though their ideas of the role bluegrass should play differed. Bluegrass was a passion for them all, but Martie and Em had spent most of their young lives studying and training to be well-rounded musicians, not just fiddlers. To be pigeonholed was the last thing either of them wanted.

Laura and Robin didn't seem worried about this. "I think we're carving our own niche," Robin told Renee Clark of *Dallas Life*. "We don't really want to conform to formula country music. We want to do what we feel in our hearts. Whether that will translate to super-stardom, I kind of doubt it. But I think as long as we're making enough money, and we're happy playing the music, who could ask for more?"

For the time being the Erwins were willing to take this Dixie Chicks ride and see where it went. Even so, the unspoken understanding between the sisters was that one day they would spread their musical wings. They believed they would have to do so if they truly wanted to see their careers take flight. The sad fact is that bluegrass tends to lose its best young players to other, more lucrative styles of music. Among the many who started in bluegrass and then moved on are Vince Gill, Keith Whitley, and Ricky Skaggs.

The self-produced first album of the Dixie Chicks, *Thank Heavens for Dale Evans*, cost $5,000 to make and was recorded at the Sumet-Bernet Studios in Dallas—which, not coincidentally, was owned by Ed Bernet, the Dixie Chicks' former booking agent. All of the songs on it are acoustic. The first cut is "The Cowboy Lives Forever," and it contains the lyrics, "There's a little bit of Roy and Dale in all of us, though all of us don't wear the cowboy boots and spurs."

The album is a mix of cover tunes and originals penned by Robin, including the melancholy ballad "Thunderheads," which many consider to be her signature song. Also included is an instrumental, "Brilliancy," arranged by Martie, which features Emily on the banjo and Laura's former Texas Rangers band mate Dave Peters on the mandolin. The title track is a musical statement from Robin disguised as a piece of country kitsch: "I'm proud enough to say that I'll always be this way, like the girl who went and stole Roy Rogers' heart."

In all, the album took two months to record, and when it was released it enjoyed modest success in the Dallas area. The group did everything possible to promote the album —even performing in schools. Shane Stein, who attended St. Mark's when Robin was still teaching there, remembers the day his seventh-grade history teacher treated her students to a live performance: she and Laura played a few songs from the album for the kids. "I don't remember exactly what they played," Shane admits, "but soon afterward I saw the full band play at a synagogue picnic, and it was a great concert."

Although it would go on to sell only 12,000 copies, the album was an important watershed for the group. It paved the way for them to attain the next level of success. Still, they found they had to be lucky as well as accomplished. As disk jockey Steve Harmon noted: "What they're doing is so different, it's not mainstream anything. It's fun to watch. But for national success, they'll need a couple of lucky breaks and a couple of lucky songs."

Not to mention stamina. While Emily and Martie juggled their academic responsibilities with touring and performing, Laura was trying to resolve the difficulties of being a single working mom. And the wear and tear of traveling from festival to festival was harder on Robin and Laura than it was on the much-younger Erwins. From the Overton Bluegrass Festival in Texas to Washington, DC's Birchmere Club, from open-air shows to Italian-restaurant performances, the Dixie Chicks spread the good musical news. It's interesting that in those early days Martie and Em hadn't yet learned to relax completely while onstage, and they often came across as serious and very shy. It was Laura who provided the comic relief; she would build up a verbal camaraderie with the audience while putting her fellow band mates at ease.

For awhile it seemed as if the Dixie Chicks might buck conventional wisdom and break through as a bluegrass band. Their profile continued to rise both inside and outside of Texas. They performed on the Nashville Network series *Nashville Now* and made their debut on *The Grand Ole Opry*. They appeared on Garrison Keillor's *Prairie Home Companion* radio show when he broadcast from Dallas in February 1991, and their

music was featured on the hit CBS series *Northern Exposure*. In 1991, they were voted Best Country Band by the *Dallas Observer* and were even hired by fast-food giant McDonald's to sing a commercial jingle. In another professional coup, they signed with Buddy Lee Attractions on Music Row for bookings, becoming the agency's only act without a recording contract.

Despite all this, the one group of people the Dixie Chicks really needed to impress—the record-label executives—seemed oblivious. The band was coming to a critical fork in the road: would they doggedly stick with their bluegrass stylings or expand their musical explorations? The answer would depend on what kind of future each member envisioned. For her part, Robin was content to stay true to her creative roots as long as she was making enough money to get by. National fame just didn't seem very important to her. Martie and Emily wanted to expand their sound—even if it was just a little bit. Laura ultimately aligned herself with the Erwin sisters, and that signaled the beginning of the end of Robin's tenure as a Dixie Chick.

When the band when back into the studio to record their second album, another independently produced effort, the tension

among the four women was apparent. Recording *Little Ol' Cowgirl* was a long, tedious, and occasionally stressful process. Each band member dealt with it in her own way. Emily, for example, brought a small trampoline to the studio so that she and the others could take mini exercise breaks and clear their heads. Sometimes they would spend their recording breaks mending their costumes.

All that tension inevitably took its toll. Everyone knew how much was riding on the success or failure of the album, so every doubt and every disagreement took on an exaggerated importance. In an interview with a local journalist Robin wearily admitted that she had spent a fair amount of time crying over her vocal tracks. Also adding to the strained atmosphere was the tacit understanding that a change of leadership was underway. Robin Lynn Macy, whose vision had originally formed and infused the group, was being slowly eased out as the Dixie Chick's front person, both literally and creatively. Laura was given the majority of the lead vocals on the new album. And, most notably, the group had begun veering away from traditional bluegrass instrumentation. True bluegrass has no drum accompaniment. Martie acknowledged that the band's second offering had "drums on every track; it's no longer bluegrass. But we have to make a living and you can't do that playing bluegrass."

Aside from Tom Van Achaik on drums, there were two more important musical additions to the album: Matthew Benjamin played guitar on several tracks, as did legendary steel guitarist Lloyd Maines. Larry Seyer, a well-known Texas producer who worked with the Dixie Chicks on *Little Ol' Cowgirl*, introduced Maines to the group. That introduction would soon change the course of Dixie Chicks history.

When Lloyd Maines was seventeen, the steel-guitar player for the Maines Brothers—a Western swing outfit that consisted of Lloyd's father and uncles—gave the teenager his old steel guitar. Lloyd was fascinated by the instrument, which had pedals that controlled the tension of the guitar strings. "It was just really intriguing all the different sounds you could get from the steel." A few years later Lloyd—along with his siblings, Steve, Kenny, and Donnie

—formed a second-generation version of the Maines Brothers. The group recorded several albums before moving on to other pursuits. By the time *Little Ol' Cowgirl* was being made Lloyd was recognized as one of the premier steel guitarists in the business.

Little Ol' Cowgirl was released in 1992. The album is a kind of small-scale version of *Rumors*, the seminal Fleetwood Mac album, in the sense that the inner turmoil of the band members is revealed through a series of emotionally raw songs. And the creative struggle being waged for the band's soul is apparent in *Little Ol' Cowgirl*'s lack of a unifying musical direction. It's a little bit bluegrass/country, a little bit country/rock and roll—as evidenced by the cover of a song by Mary Chapin Carpenter, one of the more uncountry country acts in the industry. Toss in an Irish medley and you have a musical stew that created more questions than answers for fans wondering just where the group was headed. That uncertainty preyed on Robin's mind, as well, and she would be forced to confront it sooner rather than later. What should have been a optimistic and thrilling time was tempered by the Dixie Chicks' internal creative rift.

From July 22 to 26, the group played an extended engagement at San Antonio's Fiesta Texas amusement park. Two days later, Robin announced that she was leaving the group. She claims that she literally felt the ticking of a clock. In *Chick Chat*, the group's newsletter, Robin wrote: "On July 28, 1992, after three years, my official Dixie Chicks wristwatch suddenly quit ticking. 'This must be a sign,' I gasped. It was then I knew it was time to move on and take a road less traveled. So to all my friends, thanks for the many memories. And, for now, I bid you a fond farewell."

Even in the best of circumstances the departure of a long-term band member can be a musically and emotionally difficult transition for all concerned. In this case, however, the departing musician's regret seemed greater than those of her band mates. This was because, without Robin, the Dixie Chicks were free to change directions; there would no longer be resistance from one of their own.

But while the remaining band members saw Robin's departure as an opportunity, many of their fans felt an incredible sense of loss. Leo Eilits, their buddy from the Walnut Valley Festival, says that Robin left the band, "with many regrets, but no doubts. It was an agonizing decision for her. In my opinion, she was the glue that held the original four-piece band together and molded their distinctive sound. Those who never saw the original four-piece configuration missed the incredible blend of not three, but four angelic voices performing some incredibly complex vocalizations against an acoustic background."

Yet in order to move ahead, Martie, Em, and Laura felt they had to leave a little of their history behind. Like an eternally optimistic lover, Robin chose to remain faithful to her musical roots rather than compromise what she considered to be her creative integrity. After leaving the Dixie Chicks, she took a hiatus from performing and worked as a disk jockey for the Dallas public radio station KERA 90.1 Not long after that, she teamed up with Texas folk songstress Sara Hickman and friend Patty Lege to form the Domestic Science Club, which celebrated the traditional music that Robin was so passionate about. The trio planned on recording a CD as a Christmas gift for their friends, but then a DJ they knew urged them to think bigger. They did, and their self-titled disc was released on the Discovery label.

After another release, *Three Women*, the Domestic Science Club disbanded. Robin moved back to Kansas and fell out of the public eye for awhile. She has recently resurfaced, and it's clear that she's managed to find both personal and professional peace of mind. She's formed a new group, Round Robin, and she's become a married woman. Her name is now Robin Bennett, and she continues to live in Kansas—with her husband, Mark. Along with former Danger in the Air partner Andy Owens and other notable bluegrass performers, Round Robin undertook a yearlong tour, dubbed the Bluegrass Expedition Tour. And, from the it's-a-small-world-after-all file, another member of the touring group was Troy Gilcrist, Martie and Em's old Blue Night Express partner.

After Robin's departure, Laura became the Dixie Chicks' sole lead vocalist. A guitar void also opened up when Robin left, so the band asked Matthew Benjamin, who had played on *Little Ol' Cowgirl*, to join them. They also added a drummer named Tom Van Schaik.

Hardcore Dixie Chicks fans loved *Little Ol' Cowgirl*, embracing it just the way they had *Thank Heavens for Dale Evans*. Not all the country-music critics were quite as enthusiastic, but the reviews were generally positive. The *Albuquerque Journal* noted, "The Dixie Chicks are among those who can claim their fans nationwide. Their second album helped spread the word." But, once again, the only reaction from Nashville was resounding silence.

Although *Little Ol' Cowgirl* failed to attract the attention of record-label executives, it did get through to some DJs at KYNG, Dallas's Young Country 105.3 FM, which became the first major-market commercial country station to play the Dixie Chicks. The song that was graced with airplay was "She'll Find Better Things to Do." It was truly ironic that by the time a Dixie Chicks song was finally being played on the radio Robin was no longer a member of the group. Her absence caused some confusion and discomfort. When the Dixie Chicks came out for their encore at the 1992 Balloon Festival in Plano, Texas, several audiences members shouted out for the group to perform "Thunderheads," Robin's signature tune. Momentarily at a loss, the band instead chose "Cowboy Lullabye," explaining somewhat glibly that the song "had some of the same chords." Gradually, however, the fans became accustomed to the new lineup.

With Robin gone, the remaining trio focused their energies on achieving commercial success: they wanted a recording contract, they wanted to become a national act, and they wanted to slide into mainstream country. They did not want to be a traveling band, living from gig to gig. The time had come to make a concentrated effort to attract a major label —which meant that it was time to go into the studio for the third time. It would prove to be a vastly different experience than the emotionally draining drama that resulted in *Little Ol' Cowgirl*.

This time the three band mates agreed on issues of style and sound. They set about recording in a precise and businesslike manner, determined to make the best album they could. So intent were they on getting the attention of Nashville that they decided to record their third album in Music City instead of Dallas and to feature male sidemen and songs by such Music Row favorites as Radney Foster, Kim Richey, Jamie O'Hara, and Jim Lauderdale. Then the Chicks announced that the album, to be released on the independent Crystal Clear label and produced by Lloyd Maines, would not contain any bluegrass songs. This was a bit of an exaggeration. In fact, the band had simply used the bluegrass influence in more subtle ways, such as on the title track, "Shouldn't a Told You That."

With the release of this album the Dixie Chicks saw neither their greatest fears nor their fondest hopes materialize. In retrospect *Shouldn't a Told You That* seems like a showcase album intended more for Nashville music executives than Dixie Chicks fans. And for awhile it appeared that the group had struck out on both counts. Many of their longtime fans felt that they had sold out—the very thing Robin had so passionately opposed. And, although their attempt to go more mainstream country was noticed in Nashville, not one label made an offer. One thing that worked against them was that—after Robin's departure—there were no real songwriters

in the band, so they were faced with having to record covers or tunes penned by others. Record companies prefer to invest their money in groups that are creatively self-contained. Another sticking point for some labels was the Dixie Chicks' lack of fashion sense. As long as they were still sporting those Dale Evans cowgirl ensembles, it was hard to imagine that they would be taken seriously by mainstream fans, much less the record-company people.

Despite all of this, Martie, Em, and Laura maintained their aura of optimism, but they had to know their window of opportunity was growing smaller. In their December 1993 *Chick Chat* newsletter they declared, "The newspapers and music writers are sayin' we're gettin' back to our 'country roots'— when did we ever leave? Then there's talk about Nashville lovin' it. What does all this mean? All we know is that we put our hearts into *Shouldn't a Told You That* and came up with ten new songs that we enjoyed playin'. The look of the new album, designed by nationally renowned Rex Peteet, and beautifully photographed by Carolyn McGovern, reflects our growth in the music business— hey! It's our third album! We oughta be gettin' it down right."

For the third album's release party the group rented the Granada Theater in Dallas and performed for their invited guests. "A million people showed up and had a great time while Emily and Martie presented a six-foot sandwich. There were probably a hundred record company scouts out there, but we can only see to the fifth row—so don't spoil our illusion."

The breakthrough the trio dreamed of remained elusive. But, even though they were lagging behind when it came to realizing their career goals, the Dixie Chicks were well ahead of their time in their appreciation for the power of the Internet. In an era when record and film companies were still looking upon the Internet as an enigma, the Dixie Chicks set up their own Web site. They were anxious to reach as many fans as possible, wherever possible. Besides offering the benefit of instant feedback, the Net was a cheap way to disseminate information and build a rapport with the fans. The band's early postings and newsletters were breezy and casual; they provided fans with an insight into the personalities that made up the Dixie Chicks—something the albums generally failed to do. Here, for example, is the Chicks' riff on the dean of country-music television, Ralph Emery: "When we were on *Nashville Now* recently, we were pleasantly surprised to find out that Emily wears the same shade of pancake makeup as *Ralph Emery*! We finally played Branson, Missouri—the town that has *Nytol* for breakfast. We opened for *Kenny Rogers* (he wore Lime Green)! As we rolled out of Branson, we found ourselves pondering the mind-boggling question of the ages: 'What's the difference between a Jubilee and a Jamboree?'"

Then, in early 1994, the Dixie Chicks embarked on their first European tour. Before they left town, Dallas mayor Steve Bartlett proclaimed the band the city's official music ambassadors for the duration of their tour. Their first stop was Zurich, Switzerland, a city that has its own country-music association. After completing a sold-out two-night engagement there, they flew to EuroDisney, where they performed at "Billy Bob's authentic Texas-style saloon."

The band also performed in Paris—at a venue that was quite different from those they were used to. "Our concert in Paris was at New Morning," the Chicks explained, "a

famous old listening room that was frequented by Miles Davis, and definitely intended for the serious music lover. It was an eclectic crowd due to a radio interview we shared with the world-famous Nina Hagen, a former East Berlin radical singer. We asked the poignant question, 'What do you think the reason is for the newfound popularity of country music?' Nina responded with, 'Country music has been and always will be . . . what it is.' Tres Bien, Nina."

Back in America, the band hit the road again almost immediately. They were now playing more than two hundred dates a year and learning firsthand how hard it is to maintain a personal life when you're constantly on the move. It was especially stressful for Laura, who had to leave her daughter, Asia, behind. Like working mothers everywhere, Laura worried that she'd miss seeing her child grow up. And the Erwin sisters were doing their own juggling acts. During the summer of 1994, Martie quietly planned her wedding. So low-key was her romance with Ted Seidel, a pharmaceutical-company sales rep, that none of the fans had any idea she was even engaged. Emily had a passionate but brief affair with Heath Wright of the group Ricochet. When it ended she threw herself into her work with renewed fervor; she was ready to face yet another long year of touring. Although the Dixie Chicks were in constant demand, for the most part they were still playing what many musicians would consider backwater locales. The audiences were enthusiastic and appreciative, but the three women had begun to feel that they were stuck in a career rut, spinning their creative wheels, getting nowhere fast. A change would have to be made.

The story goes that Laura walked away from the Dixie Chicks because she finally decided she couldn't sustain a life on the road away from her daughter any longer. But the truth is somewhat harsher than that. In a 1999 issue of *Country Music Magazine*, Em is quoted as saying: "Martie and I started to feel limited creatively. We felt we needed the next caliber of singer. We talked to Laura. We knew she was getting sick of not progressing further than we had. She had a teenage daughter and road life was really wearing her down. She said she didn't want to keep going unless something happened. She understood we had to make a change."

Perhaps Laura had understood intellectually, but that change was still emotionally wrenching for her. She had come so far with the band, and they could now be close to the big payoff. But the Erwin sisters were convinced there would be no big payoff unless they found the missing ingredient of their success formula. Musically, they felt they could compete with anyone: but vocally, they were out of the running. A band's lead vocalist often establishes its musical personality, and Laura's contribution just wasn't quite forceful enough.

While working with the Dixie Chicks on *Shouldn't a Told You That*, Lloyd Maines had given Em and Martie a copy of his daughter Natalie's audition tape for the prestigious Berklee School of Music in Boston. Natalie had been singing since she was three, and she possessed a powerful voice. According to Dixie Chick lore, both Erwin sisters had copies of the tape in their cars, and each had independently come to the conclusion that Natalie would make a perfect Dixie Chicks lead vocalist. So, even as they discussed a parting of the ways with Laura, the Erwins already had her replacement in mind. "We knew we weren't going to leave each other

high and dry," Emily still insisted, speaking to journalist Robert Oermann. "Martie and I really started thinking about what we wanted. We were really at the point where we were wanting that major-label success."

After Laura had officially resigned, Martie and Em called Natalie Maines. She was ready for them. "I had always loved watching them play," recalls Natalie, "but I was not impressed at all with the singing. I had been waiting for my shot." Because Lloyd had played on the Dixie Chicks' second album and produced and played on their third, the Maines household was very familiar with Dixie Chicks music—although, as Natalie acknowledges, "My mom had listened to their music more than I did. When I went to see them live, I was blown away by how well they could play their instruments." Somewhat unbelievably, Natalie claims that she had no idea she was being auditioned for the lead singing spot until Emily started peppering her with questions like, "Would you ever be interested in singing country music? Would you be interested in moving to Dallas?" Natalie went back to her studies at Texas Tech and waited to hear more from the Erwins. Martie and Em didn't need to deliberate very long: they loved Natalie's voice, and they also felt she had the right background for the job. "Because her dad was on the road her whole life, we knew Natalie understood the lifestyle."

About a week later, the Erwins called and asked Natalie if she would consider dropping out of college, moving to Dallas, and learning thirty songs in four days. Not only did she leave college, but she also walked away from a full scholarship at Berklee. Yet she never looked back. Now, says Natalie, she sees "how brave Martie and Emily were to do this. When you go back and listen to what they were doing three years ago, you see how much it has changed."

In an interview with Mario Tarradell of the *Dallas Morning News*, Martie defended the band's evolution, describing it as a natural process: "If you think about the fact that Emily was sixteen and I was nineteen when the band started, and think about your life when you're in your late twenties, how much change you go through from sixteen to twenty-five, from the time you're nineteen to the time you're twenty-eight, those are your growing years. The music has naturally changed just based on where we were at in our lives. Emily and I have always been either half of the band or two-thirds of the band. That's why we carried these traditions of the banjo solos, the dobro solos and the fiddle solos that have kept it a Chick thing, the Chick sound."

In the spring 1996 *Chick Chat* newsletter, Laura's resignation was announced to the fans. "Last fall, our dear friend Laura Lynch left the band to pursue other life adventures. And so one chapter ends . . . Goodbye Laura." In parting, Laura wrote to her fans and supporters: "Seven years. We had some wonderful times. You gave up your Friday and Saturday nights just to come hear our band. I was always so flattered. Touched. I will miss those times. I will miss you."

However, when talking to *Dallas Morning News* columnist Helen Bryant, Laura used a different tone. Bryant wrote:

"Here a chick . . . This item could be a country song: 'Two Chicks Dumped Me for a Younger Woman.' Laura Lynch has been replaced as lead singer of the Dixie Chicks by Natalie Maines, the daughter of steel guitarist Lloyd Maines. Sisters Emily Erwin and Martie Seidel—the other two Chicks—hope Natalie's powerful voice will propel the trio to commercial success.

'We thought we needed to make a music decision now,' says Martie, adding that Laura views the change as 'the passing of the baton.' But when I talked to Laura Wednesday night, she sounded awful fond of that ol' baton.

'It can't really be characterized as a resignation,' Laura said. 'There are three Dixie Chicks, and I'm only one.' She said age was a factor in the baton-passing, and she understands. 'The group's called the Dixie Chicks,' said Laura, who's 37. (Emily and Martie are 23 and 25, respectively.) 'When I was out there on the road having a bad day, it was awfully hard to be a Chick.' The upside for Laura: 'I have a 14-year-old daughter, and I'm looking forward to spending more time with her.'"

While memories of her days as a Dixie Chick still trigger bittersweet emotions, life has been good to Laura since she left the group. Not long after her resignation—forced or otherwise—she married her high-school sweetheart, rancher Mac Tull, and moved to a

spread outside the west Texas town of Weatherford. Laura still attends bluegrass festivals, although she hasn't returned to performing.

The same issue of *Chick Chat* that contained Laura's farewell also featured Natalie's introduction: "And another chapter begins—Natalie Maines, Lubbock native and daughter of world famous producer and steel guitar player Lloyd Maines, has added her exciting new voice to the Dixie Chicks. We are truly honored to have her as a part of the dream! 'Howdy y'all [writes Natalie]. 'I just wanted to say thank you to all the fans who have so graciously welcomed me as the new "Chick" in the coop. Since last Fall I have been having a great time. Everything is so new and exciting, and I hope to meet all of you down the road. Until then.'"

With Natalie on board, the entire dynamic of the group changed. First of all, she was not a traditionalist by anyone's standards. Her influences leaned more towards the Indigo Girls than Mark O'Connor. In fact, she had grown up dreaming of being a rock star but later discovered that her voice didn't lend itself to that genre. Even so, she was young and in tune with the contemporary commercial sound. Plus she brought a raw energy to the mix that the graceful Laura hadn't possessed. Emily and Martie's musicianship fueled the Dixie Chicks engine, while Natalie was the spark plug. She was also outspoken. When agreeing to join the band she put forward a stipulation: the clothes and hair had to go. "The only thing I knew for sure was that I wasn't going to wear those cowgirl clothes."

Way back when, the cowgirl motif had seemed like a lark, but by now it had become a liability, something that diminished the band's music in the eyes of many label executives. "We wanted to get out of that gimmicky thing," Em admits. "We were at a point

where we really wanted the music to speak for itself." So the arrival of Natalie coincided with the dawn of a new fashion sense—out went the beads and the fringe and in came the lace and the slit skirts. And with this bolder look came a bolder sound, which, seemingly overnight, vaulted the Dixie Chicks to a new level of musical validity.

The change was noticed almost immediately. Of course not everyone welcomed it. Leo Eilits, who had been among the first to hear the original Dixie Chicks, mourned the passing of an era. "Like many of the people who knew them during the early days of the band and before, we are very proud of our little sisters, but we view their recent success with some regret. The Bluegrass community, where they cut their teeth and polished their instrumental skills, no longer has access to their sparkling performances, and we miss them."

In the midst of this career transition, change was also taking place on the personal front. Martie and Em's mom and dad divorced, and Barbara Erwin married Farrel Trask, who became a beloved second dad to the girls and one of their biggest supporters. In June 1995 Martie finally married Ted Seidel. He had proposed on Vail Mountain, determined not to let Martie's career take her away from him. Ted had a young son, Carter, from a previous marriage, so not only did Martie find herself a newlywed, but also a mom with a ready-made family to think about. Natalie was dating guitarist Michael Tarabay, who would soon propose marriage as well. Only Emily was free of romantic involvement, and she continued to devote all her energies to promoting the Dixie Chicks and playing her music. A few years later, however, Em would become engaged to singer-songwriter Charlie Robison.

Natalie worked hard to transform herself into a Dixie Chick, she even learned to play guitar. But few who saw her first performances with the group—such as the one at the inaugural gala for the governor of Texas—could believe that she wasn't a longtime Chick. Almost from their first rehearsal, the three women displayed a magical chemistry. It infused the group with a new power, a musical distinctiveness. As word spread about the Chicks' new look, Nashville power brokers sat up and took notice. At long last, Music Row came calling. But, after having waited for so long, Martie and Emily weren't about to let any record executive tamper with who they were.

Prior to Laura's departure, Sony Music had checked the group out, but the company hadn't been inspired to approach the trio with an offer. In 1996 Sony took another look; this time any doubts were laid to rest. Sony now wanted to sign the Dixie Chicks as the flagship act for its planned revival of the Monument label, which had been the home of such legendary country acts as Dolly Parton, Willie Nelson, Kris Kristofferson, and Connie Smith back in the sixties and seventies.

The Sony/Dixie Chicks negotiations were a drawn-out affair, although there were apparently no tense moments or potential deal-breakers. The Erwins insisted that they be allowed to maintain their signature sound—meaning the dobro, fiddle, mandolin, and banjo would stay—and they were pleasantly surprised when Sony readily agreed to that demand. There was some concern about the group's name—Sony was worried that the moniker "Dixie Chicks" would be perceived as politically incorrect by a certain segment of the record-buying public, but the label eventually agreed to let it go.

In the end, the deal took five months to hammer out. The Dixie Chicks, in return for being permitted to keep their name, had to agree to a six-album deal. While on the one hand the deal appeared to provide the Dixie Chicks with a stable home base and financial security, on the other hand it legally bound them to the company, regardless of how Sony promoted their music. Still, it was too good to pass up, and so the deal was signed.

During this time Natalie married Michael Tarabay, but she didn't have much time to sit back and enjoy being a newlywed. Within a month of closing the deal with Sony the Dixie Chicks were back in the recording studio, this time backed by big-label resources. A do-it-now-or-die pressure was bearing down on them. They embarked on the project with four songs already selected and a plan to cut eight tracks in all. Once the four preselected tracks—including "You Were Mine," penned by Em and Martie—were in the can, they would choose the remaining material and then record it. Of the first group of songs, the one that seemed most suitable for release as a single was "I Can Love You Better," which would become the group's first single for Sony and their first song to be made into a video. Before the album itself became available, Sony wanted to release a single to gauge audience reaction and to generate some buzz about the group. As strange as it may seem

today, many within Sony at that point considered the Dixie Chicks an alternative country group with limited appeal. In a year's time, of course, they would be revising their opinion.

The Dixie Chicks' major-label debut single and video were showcased at the Hastings Music Convention, an industry showcase held at Nashville's famed Ryman Auditorium. Although it wasn't really number-one material, "I Can Love You Better" did get radio airplay, and the video allowed the fans a glimpse of the new-look Chicks. For the most part, the reception the reinvented Dixie Chicks received was better than Sony could have hoped for. However, the band did experience some negative feedback from their old bluegrass fans, some of whom were shocked at the sight of Natalie's punkish hair and Madonna-esque wardrobe. Natalie took it all in her stride: "I look at it like I just get to live this life once and if I can't live it being myself then that's kind of a shame. I mean, I get myself in trouble sometimes, but it's worth it, because I'm not going to be something that I'm not. And I think that's one thing that people our age can relate to as well."

For Martie, however, the backlash was painful, even though she knew that she and her sister had done what was right for them. Had they not changed direction it was quite possible that Martie would have given up. "I had contemplated leaving the group," she later revealed. "I told my husband, 'Musically, my growth is being stunted. I can't play bluegrass and cowgirl music forever. I can't wear these gawd-awful spangles and rhinestones forever! I've got to make a change, [even if] that's having babies and giving fiddle lessons the rest of my life.'"

So, in some respects, Natalie Maines rescued the Dixie Chicks. Then Lloyd Maines gave them their final boost into stardom. In 1997, Lloyd had produced an album for an Amarillo sextet called the Groobees. On that disc was a song written by Groobees lead singer Susan Gibson called "Wide Open Spaces," a bittersweet tune about a daughter leaving home. Naturally, Lloyd thought of his own daughter when he first heard the song—because of the tune's sentimental lyrics and because he knew what she could do with the song as a performer—so he sent Natalie a copy of the track. Not only did she, Em, and Martie fall in love with the song, but Sony did also. It became both the title track of the Dixie Chicks' latest album and the next single to be released from it. *Wide Open Spaces* finally hit the market in January of 1998.

When the time came to shoot the video for the single "Wide Open Spaces," the band chose a Rockies location; the cameras would roll at West Fest, an annual event hosted by Michael Martin Murphy. The Chicks had performed there the previous four years, and shooting their video at the fest was their way of thanking Murphy for his support; for one thing, he had scheduled them between big-name acts to showcase their talents. The Erwins wanted people to know that whatever the future held for them they weren't about to forget those who had stood behind them over the years.

Wide Open Spaces received solid reviews. One critic described the group as a "country Wilson Philips with those lush, tight stylings, though they spice the proceedings with a touch of blues." Although the album didn't charge out of the gate, the Dixie Chicks began to enjoy great word of mouth. Each new single strengthened their standing among Nashville's elite acts. Almost a year after its release, *Wide Open Spaces* would top the country charts. It would eventually yield five hit singles and become the bestselling album by a country group to date. Country music had discovered its next "overnight" superstars.

It meant a lot to the Chicks that they had managed to sell more albums in Texas than anywhere else. "We rode the Nashville-Texas line and kept our signature sound," Emily said in an interview with Stephanie Dale of Australia's *Country Update*. "We also kept the

radio market in mind and I don't think we compromised anything. We really tried hard not to sound too slick, and it was important to us to play our own instruments. For some reason Nashville sees the banjo as too hokey, too down home." Emily went on to explain that the banjo is "bluegrass, it's hillbilly, and Nashville is trying so hard to be hip that sometimes it leaves behind its roots. So it was fun insisting on the banjo. We were very straightforward about what we wanted, and Sony knew where we were coming from, and they let us color outside the lines."

In July 1998 "There's Your Trouble," became the group's first number-one single. That September they made their debut as Country Music Association Award nominees a memorable one by taking home both the prestigious Horizon Award for career development and the Vocal Group of the Year prize. Prior to the awards show, which was telecast on CBS, Martie suffered a bad case of nerves. She told USA Today's Brian Mansfield, "I used to sit on my bed with my own ballot sheet, drinking Diet Coke and eating Chee-tos. I had my whole party on my bed, watching the CMA Awards, probably the last ten years of my life." Those days were over. Now Martie herself would be a vital part of the ceremonies.

While most industry insiders believed that the Dixie Chicks would win the Horizon Award hands down, few thought the newcomers stood a chance to take the Vocal Group of the Year title; they were up against the likes of perennial winner Alabama and such established acts as Diamond Rio, Sawyer Brown, and the Mavericks. The fact that *Wide Open Spaces* had outsold the offerings of all the other contenders was not considered enough. That's why so many people—particularly the Chicks themselves—were shocked when the winner was announced. "My heart stopped beating when they called our name," said Emily. "I didn't know what to do, and my fiancé [Charlie Robison] started hugging me and saying, 'I'm so proud of you.'" During their acceptance speech, Martie emotionally acknowledged Sony: "Thanks for letting us color outside the lines."

According to Ed Benson, executive director of the Country Music Association, it was their unique colors that set the Dixie Chicks apart. "You have a vocal group with three females, and that hasn't really existed in our business before," he told Mario Tarradell of the *Dallas Morning News*. "Then their personalities have brought edge and attitude, and edge and attitude have been playing pretty well in our business lately. And musically, here's a group that's very credible. These ladies are talented musicians. Playing up that attitude and that edge with the female-power thing in our society allows them to interest the female buying public, and the females buy sixty percent of the country records today. And they are physically attractive enough to interest the males." But, warned Benson, the Dixie Chicks are not "the Spice Girls of country music. This is an act that has substantial musical credibility. That is inherently necessary in country music."

If being named Vocal Group of the Year was an honor, then winning the Horizon Award was a vote of confidence. "The Horizon Award meant so much to us because it means the industry has faith in you and feels like you'll have some longevity," Emily told Anika Van Wyk of the *Calgary Sun*.

The same year, the Dixie Chicks also won Country Music Television's Rising Star Award, and they were lauded by many critics for having produced one of the best albums of the year. But, for all the success and critical acclaim they enjoyed in 1998, their breakout year, the following year would see them become firmly established, not just as a top country act but also one of the more popular groups in the entire music business. Despite their steadily increasing mainstream appeal, however, the Chicks retained their left-of-center way of doing things. For instance, Natalie suggested that each Chick get a chicken foot tattooed on her own foot for every gold record and number-one single the group achieved. "We said, 'Yeah, sure,' thinking it was way down the line," Em told *People*'s Jeremy Helligar. "Then five months later we were going gold, and we said, 'Oh, no! We're getting a tattoo!'"

Now that their struggle to be accepted by Nashville was over, Martie and Emily seemed more relaxed both onstage and off, showing glimpses of the humor and companionship that held them and their musical enterprise together. During an interview with Gary McCollum of *University Wire*, Martie teased, "Emily and I have wanted to do this [play country music] since we first saw those gals pop out of the cornfield on *Hee Haw*. Emily

almost tried out for the show when we first came to Nashville, but they didn't seem to need any 32 As." To which Emily responded by laughing and saying, "Pay back is hell, Martie."

They may have hoped life would slow down when they achieved success, but the three Chicks found their schedules more hectic than ever. Except that now, instead of playing backwater towns, they were touring with, and opening for, some of the biggest names in country music, such as George Straight. In their minds it was better to be an opening act than a headliner while still introducing their music to new fans—and reintroducing it to fans of the earlier Chicks incarnations. Ego had never been a driving force for the Dixie Chicks, and it wasn't about to become one now. All they cared about was nurturing their music and connecting with their audience.

It also wasn't long before Hollywood also came a-calling. The Dixie Chicks were asked to contribute two songs to the soundtrack of the film *Runaway Bride*, starring Richard Gere and Julia Roberts: "Ready to Run" and a cover of "You Can't Hurry Love." And, through it all, the awards kept piling up. In February of 1999 the group was voted Favorite New Country Artist at the American Music Awards; then, the following month, they shook the Grammy Awards by taking home statues for Best Country Performance ("There's Your Trouble") and Best Country Album (*Wide Open Spaces*). At the Academy of Country Music Awards they again cleaned up, taking three coveted prizes: Best New Vocal Duo or Group, Top Vocal Duo/Group, and Album of the Year.

While all these kudos served to validate the Chicks as performers, they also created huge expectations for them to satisfy when it came time to record their next album. But rather than letting themselves get trapped inside the what-if-we-screw-up pressure cooker, Martie, Natalie, and Emily decided to just do the music that appealed to them and have faith that the audience would follow. "If you spend so much time worrying about it, I think it taints the well of what you're trying to do," explained Natalie. "If you add in worry and uneasiness about doing the right thing, then that automatically is the opposite of who we are and what we do."

Success can bring interesting new opportunities. Somewhat surprisingly, the group was asked to participate in the final Lilith Fair. To organizer Terry McBride, however, the Dixie Chicks seemed a logical choice. The Lilith Fair people were interested in acts that had an established sales base; they also wanted performers who were capable, in McBride's words, of "adding something new and breaking down barriers. Obviously, the Chicks have all those things."

What the Chicks also had was a wedding to attend. In May of 1999, Emily married her cowboy, Charlie Robison, and for the occasion Martie wrote a song called "Cowboy Take Me Away." The inspiration for the song's title came from a Calgon bath oil commercial, and the lyrics expressed how much Martie loved her sister's free spirit. But while Emily's love life had taken a happy turn, Natalie's marriage to Michael Tarabay had ended badly after just eighteen months. "I felt like I could take a breath, finally, after a year and a half," Natalie told Chris Willman of *Entertainment Weekly*. "Maybe just once every few weeks when I get a call from my lawyer do I ever remember I'm married. So the divorce didn't occupy my mind at all during the making of the album. There's no sappy songs about leaving." That's probably because Natalie was furious over money issues surrounding the divorce. Soon, however, she was in recovery mode: at Em's wedding Natalie told her friends that she had found a new love. "Someone who treats me right for once. I had very low expectations of love—and life—and now they're back up. To fantasy! Which is where I think they should be."

In August of 1999, the Dixie Chicks' second album for Sony was released. The group had originally wanted to call it *Sin Wagon*, but they were overruled by nervous label executives, many of whom still couldn't figure out exactly where the Chicks were coming from. So the album was titled *Fly*, instead, which turned out to be prophetic—once again, sales soared. Amazingly, the women who had launched their careers with a "Stand by Your Man" look had turned into country feminists. "We're hoping to do things by example, not by some sort of motto or some big philosophical statement," Emily told *USA Weekend*'s Jennifer Mendelsohn. "Our music and what we do, touring and running our own company, hopefully inspires young girls to go out and do whatever *they* want to do."

Of course, independent-minded people who strive to set an example often find themselves in hot water. *Fly* generated both quadruple-platinum sales and a certain amount of controversy. The video for the single "Goodbye Earl" depicts an abused wife who enlists the help of a friend to kill her husband. Although the subject matter is dark and very serious, the video plays it for laughs—of the uneasy and irreverent variety. The Chicks performed the song on the February 2000 Grammy Awards telecast while a clip from the video played on an overhead screen. It featured a star-studded cast, including NYPD *Blue* star Dennis Franz as the villainous Earl. The Chicks, big fans of both Franz and the police drama, personally asked the Emmy Award-winning actor to appear in the clip after meeting him during a *Rosie O'Donnell Show* taping. Also appearing in the video were *Ally McBeal*'s actress Jane Krakowski as Wanda, the terrorized wife, and *Chicago Hope*'s Lauren Holly as Maryann, Wanda's true-blue friend. Natalie's new boyfriend, film actor Adrian Pasdar, put in an appearance as an investigative cop.

Despite the video's playful tone, the Dixie Chicks wanted to make it clear that they believe there is nothing funny about domestic violence. "We took a serious subject and did it in a way that makes it a little bit easier to listen to," explained Emily. "Sometimes songs get so serious that they make people very uncomfortable. 'Earl' is meant to be light-hearted and fun, and if in the process it brings a serious subject into the forefront, then that's great. We're not promoting murder, and we even say that in a disclaimer on our album—besides, is there a gentler way to go than with black-eyed peas?" Their approach seemed to hit a nerve, because the National Coalition Against Domestic Violence released a statement supporting the clip and lauding the trio for raising public awareness of an urgent problem. Oh, and as for the Grammys themselves, the Dixie Chicks walked off with awards for Best Country Performance for "Ready to Run," and *Fly* was named Best Country Album. Once again, the Chicks ruled the nest.

Now, having hit their first two Sony albums out of the park, the Dixie Chicks plan to regroup and create more music for their legion of fans to enjoy. Professionally, it's an exciting time for the trio, but the success they've achieved continues to demand certain personal sacrifices. Career pressures finally undermined Martie's marriage to the point where

she and her husband, Ted Seidel, filed for divorce. Although she's very much in the limelight these days, Martie is trying to keep the divorce proceedings as private as possible for the sake of her stepson, Carter.

The Dixie Chicks, individually and collectively, feel the heat. The industry and the audiences have high expectations of them now that they've achieved superstar status; and Emily, Martie, and Natalie also expect a lot of themselves. Still, as Natalie insists, they won't squander their energies fretting about whether they'll remain in fashion from one year to the next. "I don't have any fear," she declares, "not because I believe that we'll be around forever or anything. I just believe you can't worry about stuff like that. We make the music that we want to make and we hope the public accepts it and we're very grateful if they do, but we can't base our entire careers [on] making other people happy. They're either gonna like it or they're not. If they don't like it, then I believe that it means that it's time to just let it be, and that's obviously the path that's been chosen for us."

But the Dixie Chicks seem unlikely to be walking down that path anytime soon.

dixiechicks

Sources

Brooks, Robert. *All Inclusive Dixie Chicks Page*.
 dixiechicks.mixedsignal.net/

Bryant, Helen. "My, Look Who's Coming to Dallas; Chick Memories Recall
 the Best and the Worst of Times." *Dallas Morning News*, 16 Oct. 1995.

Chick Chat [Dixie Chicks online newsletter]. Dec. 1993; spring 1995.
 www.Dixie-Chicks.com/cchat.html

Clark, Renee. *Dallas Life Magazine* 1 Mar. 1992.

Dale, Stephanie. Interview with the Dixie Chicks. *Country Update* [Australia]
 Nov. 1998.

Helligar, Jeremy, with Chris Rose. "Feather Friends with a Platinum Album
 and a No. 1 Single . . ." *People* 28 Sept. 1998.

Rev. of *Little Ol' Cowgirl*, by the Dixie Chicks. *Albuquerque Journal* 13 Sept. 1992.

McCollum, Gary. "Dixie Dynamos." *University Wire* 31 Aug. 1998.
 Kentucky Kernel via U-Wire. www.u-wire.com

Mendelsohn, Jennifer. "Sexy Yet Serious: These Aren't Spice Chicks . . ."
 USA Weekend 11 Nov. 1998.

Tarradell, Mario. "Dixie Chicks Are Rare Birds Indeed." *Dallas Morning News*
 10 Apr. 1998.

—. "These Days, Success Is a Relative . . ." *Dallas Morning News* 25 Jan. 1998.

Van Wyk, Anika. "Chicks Are Diggin' It . . ." *Calgary Sun* 18 Nov. 1998.

Willman, Chris. "Whistlin' Dixies . . ." *Entertainment Weekly* 9 Mar. 1999.